From the Ground Up

Pat Skinner

ISBN 979-8-89428-521-4 (paperback)
ISBN 979-8-89428-522-1 (digital)

Christian Faith Publishing
832 Park Avenue
Meadville, PA 16335
www.christianfaithpublishing.com

Printed in the United States of America

CONTENTS

PROLOGUE

I NEVER PLANNED ON WRITING A book about my life. I have done several others on different topics and have designed one large coloring book in the hippie days. This is something new. A venture such as this doesn't involve a lot of research, only the assembling of dates, times, and events to the best of my recollection. So I must ask myself: What is the purpose of this writ? What goal am I trying to achieve? To me, it is just my life or experiences, and everybody has one along with their own experiences.

For most of my life, I have just seen people as people—some jerks, good or bad. I am not really an egotistical person, so what would the purpose be in sharing my story with someone else?

I have had good, bad, happy, sad, easy, and tough times, the same as another person. In light of all that, that is where we are equal. So on with the show, and as you go through the chapters of my life and experiences, I pray you will find the goal, point, and purpose I am aiming at and trying to achieve.

May the Lord bless you!

In His love,
Pat Skinner

INTRODUCTION

FIRST: HOW DO I BEGIN a venture such as this? Would it be as follows?

It was a brisk, cold, and windy morning in 1956. The wind chill was below zero as I was waiting for the bus at the corner across from my house. The bus arrived after around a ten-minute wait, which seemed like hours. Here it came; the bus was there. Great! Now it was warmer inside. Only upon entering, the only thing lost was the wind chill and my view of my mom waving out from the frosted window of our home in small-town Minnesota. The inside of that bus was like the inside of a freezer in a locker plant, with the sound of the small heater whizzing with a loose fan blade. We were the first kids to be picked up. Now we were pulling away, and the picture of the stop and my mom waving from the window were but memories. I was on my way to a new school, St. Mary's. I was previously in Washington before. Now the memory came back; I wonder if they have blocks there that are so big—nearly three feet tall and around six feet when stacked. I don't know. What I do remember was that I fell off and had to be treated because I landed on my head. (Wow, did something start there?)

Anyway, it got warmer as more kids got on the bus. Now we were making our stops, dropping kids off at their schools. I saw Mike Nelson, my neighbor, walking toward the door of his school as we were now on the home stretch to mine a few blocks away. I didn't know at the time that in four or five years we would be having fistfights as well as pellet gun fights with four or five of his friends and three of mine. It is amazing how we sometimes never see what is in the future—good or bad, learning or not learning, and what it might bring.

This is where I arrived today. I never planned on writing a book in the future, which is now. I have started a couple of times in the past forty years.

My dad said once after I was arrested for being drunk and was parked with a girl who was eighteen or nineteen. I was fifteen or so, and all he said was, "There is a time and place for everything."
So I believe this is the time to write this book.

CHAPTER 1

THE EARLY YEARS

IN THE SUMMER OF 1949, June to be exact, I entered this world kicking and screaming. Yes, in a small town in the northwestern corner of Minnesota, I came forth with my own ideas, seeking city life. I had no idea of what I was going to be subjected to. I was oblivious to what was happening. My dad was a military man and retired as a master sergeant later on after over twenty years in the service. He had a field commission and received the rank of major also. My mother was an avid reader, as well as my dad. They always would say, as far back as I can recall, "Always find the facts and hear both sides of the story first."

Dad became a recruiting agent after World War II, and that is how we ended up in Thief River Falls, Minnesota. I had two older brothers who died early, then I came along. My dad was transferred occasionally, as they do in the military, so we moved several times. We were in Austin, Mankato, and finally, the family ended up in Willmar, Minnesota, where Dad retired. He liked the woods and fishing, and Willmar had a number of surrounding lakes, so he stayed there. My brother Mike was born, and Dad always took us hunting and fishing with him as we grew. Mom was also into fishing and hunting. We would go after squirrels, ducks, pheasants, rabbits, and deer. I had my own gun before I was twelve and was taught gun safety and how to properly tear one down and clean it after use. If you went hunting, you cleaned and ate your game; you didn't just shoot something to shoot it. The same with fish. You were taught to respect nature and the lakes.

In the fifties, you could shoot hawks and crows, so we would occasionally get one of them. My dad was into taxidermy and would mount some of these birds. Mom would only go after ducks and pheasants, and once in a while, she'd go deer hunting. My mother was into all areas of sports. She held titles in golf after we grew older, along with tennis, and bowling, and she was active later in racquetball, badminton, and softball, where she was a pitcher. She was active in starting women's sports in the county we lived in, in the early seventies. She was a writer of sports articles in the paper. The only sports my dad did with her were fishing and hunting, and he bowled for a while. He never opposed her doing these things. Neither were drinkers, and your family came first, along with the church. Both were more concerned about your character than how you made them look. Some parents I have seen would always say, "Do you know how you make us look?" Ours never did that. They would say, "Do you know what you are doing to yourself?" I like that now. They were concerned about you.

I have six brothers and sisters. Each one of us has had our own business throughout the years. We were taught to read and apply what we learned and never lose our integrity. Stand for what you believe. I thank God we had been taught a good code of morals or pointed in that direction anyway. It is a display of good character. My dad, after retiring from the military, became the veterans' service representative for the county and did that for the next twenty years. He cared about the veterans, their families, and widows. The previous officer had a drinking problem and couldn't maintain the job. He was one of my dad's friends, and Dad tried to help him, but Chuck just couldn't keep it together. He told Dad to apply, and he got the job. Chuck still owned the go-cart track and skating rink in Spicer, ten miles from Willmar. We could go there and drive carts for free once in a while, which was cool. He was a nice guy, but the drink just got to him. Later, I recognized Dad wasn't against drinking, but if it affected your responsibility, you stayed away from it.

My parents were always home at night, and Mom, as the kids got older, got out more for bowling, golf, and the like. Prior to this, she would have the girls, as she said, coming over for the bridge.

They would go to a different house each month, play cards, eat lunch, and have coffee, never alcohol. Each of them had children, and they would go home to be there when the kids got home. My dad was the cook on the weekends so Mom could watch her sports. Dad would go hunting or take care of things around the house or yard. Responsibility came first. I learned more from this example than anything.

When my dad retired from the Veterans' service, he recommended another person for the job other than his assistant. His assistant was too often late for work or had been up all night playing cards and drinking. He felt he wouldn't be the best for the veterans and could possibly not be reliable on the job. Dad had seen this with Chuck when he was the officer for the vets. You did your best and were to be on the job for the people you were responsible for. This is where I have seen his standing for what he believed. During this time, and because of his decision to recommend another for the job, Dad was harassed, criticized, and condemned for his decision.

Mom and Dad would go out occasionally on Friday for dinner and dancing. They were very good dancers, I must say. But after the problems with people harassing them, they couldn't do that anymore for some time. It was awful. He just accepted that is the way they are without knowing the facts. He practiced understanding the facts. He didn't sit and complain about it all the time like some do. He stayed home and still helped some of the vets after he retired. He got involved also in helping disabled and terminally ill children. Like both would say, get out of yourself and do something for someone else.

The example I had growing up was, I believe, a very good one. It is something like that old saying, you never know the love of a parent till you become one yourself. Both my parents had earned a number of awards for service and winning competitions. These things never came overnight, as some might want them to. They come over time through being consistent and growing as you grow. My parents grew up with us. In hearing about the ways and character of my folks, it may almost sound like we were the Cleavers or something. That definitely was and is not the case. Dad had a number of little sayings taped up to the kitchen cabinet doors, such as one he had forever as it seems. It goes thusly:

> This is the beginning of a new day. God has given me this day to use as I will. I can waste it, or use it for good. What I do today is very important because I am exchanging a day of my life for it. When tomorrow comes this day will be gone forever leaving something in its place I have traded for it. I want gain not loss, good not evil, success not failure. In order that I shall not forget the price I paid for it. (Author unknown)

I saw how my dad valued his family. When I was in my rebellious years, I couldn't wait till I was sixteen to quit school. The years before, I had been kicked out. If I could quit, I would be legal. I came home, and that night my dad said, "Remember, now you think you're an adult. First, your mom may be your mother, but don't forget she is my wife." I was to pay my mom twenty dollars a month for washing my clothes if she did. They must be ready and by the washer, or they don't get done. I could eat supper there if I was on time, and he would pay the electricity and the utilities. It wasn't a free ride. I came and went pretty much as I pleased, and usually came home drinking. This didn't fly. No girls staying over or coming in. It was a good value in relation to morals and character.

> Foolishness is found in the heart of a child, but the rod of correction shall drive it far from him. (Proverbs 22:15)

I was a rebel. These values and the example gave me a foundation to return to after my days of folly. I notice many parents today do not adhere to many of these values. They are concerned about how the child is always feeling. There is a fine line here. It is not abuse to set an example and stick to your guns. Children have no idea what life is about from life experiences. Especially if they are smart, they still don't understand what the consequences are. I never saw my dad put my mother down or criticize her. They spoke about things in private. They never complained about money in front of the kids. This creates insecurity, as I later found out. We were never put down or called stupid. Sometimes we were told it was a ridiculous decision. Never called an idiot. Usually, it was something like, "You are smarter than that." This, I found out, helped us not condemn ourselves.

Mom was a fluent musician. She had been around music her whole life, as my grandpa had played with Lawrence Welk. He played violin. Mom played violin, organ, piano, and trumpet. She also got into guitar, drums, and banjo. We always had music, a big band, and an orchestra, and listened to the Ink Spots, Kingston Trio, and more. She would always be singing and listening to some album after she got a stereo. Later, I became interested in music along with my artwork. I took trumpet lessons and piano until the nun teaching piano beat my hands with a rod for not holding them correctly during one of the lessons. That was the beginning of a problem later on.

Dad was not a musical person, but he liked it. Mom would play Harry James stuff and the like. When we were jamming, Dad never said it was stupid or to shut up. He would just say, "Can you take a break while I read the paper?" Our living room at one time looked like a studio. We had a PA, organ, piano, guitars on stands, clarinets, trumpets, flutes, and drums along with several microphones with stands. Oh, can't forget the banjos and guitars with harmonicas. It was fun.

In the midst of all this, there were seven children. I was the oldest. Because of so many, we would have family meetings on Friday night. These were so if you had a complaint against someone in the family, we could get it out into the open. We really had no secrets. I didn't like it because they were after supper, and I wanted to go and party with my friends. What I see now is my dad putting effort into keeping order and being an example of a peacemaker in the family. This was a great example again. Did I notice it then? I don't think so.

I had already been busted for drinking a couple of times, gotten into trouble in school for fighting, and was fifteen and thought I knew everything.

> Train up a child in the way he should go,
> and when he is old, he will not depart from it.
> (Proverbs 22:6)

Well, as we all know, there is a time period between the training and the returning. We evidently return when we find out our own ways and ideas don't work. I am very blessed to have had a base to return to through the example set by my parents. One thing I discovered is both parties must work together. This is something rare these days. Individual rights seem to be more important than the family unit as a whole. One party is not treated right; they are focused on their careers. Some discuss adult issues with children who have no knowledge or life experiences. This is foolish. Maybe that is why so many are protesting different causes they don't even understand.

> Children's children are the crown of old
> men; and the glory of children are their fathers.
> (Proverbs 17:6)

I see it as the father's responsibility to lead the family. In some cases, the wife or woman won't let him. In some, the father won't even get involved with God or the Bible. It is leading the family spiritually in the way God has designed, not a tyrant like some religious people are. It is through love.

Part of the training was the example, of how he reacted and what he did. He was rough in some areas, which I will cover later. However, his consistency with what he did is what he said. "Do as I do," and he did it.

We each had a part in the home. Each had a job according to our age and abilities. We started by cleaning our room and making our bed. "Your mother is not your maid." We washed dishes, and Dad took the time to show us how to do it with hot water and soap.

You know the routine. "Clear the plates from the table as soon as you are done eating." Some people, it seems, never have had this. They leave stuff all over the place.

When we got a little older, we got jobs. I started selling donuts door-to-door, paper routes, and walked or rode bikes unless it was really bad weather. When I was a little older, I got a job working for some farmers. Here I baled hay, cleaned barns, and helped some friends who raised Morgan horses clean the barns. I rode horses a lot then. At about the same time, on weekends, I would caddy at the golf course for the tournaments, and for a few weeks in the summer, I would help pick cucumbers. We were always busy. We didn't have a lot of money, and with seven kids, it is expensive.

I began doing oil paintings and illustrations when I was eleven, and when I reached fourteen, I was already doing poster art and signs for the hospital doings around town. I had done artwork and drawings for a small paper called the Reminder in Willmar. But on weekends, when I was fifteen, we met at the Blue Chip Cafe, and I would draw and paint T-shirt designs like the Ed Roth ones you see. I also did jackets and shirts for some of the gangs, as well as pin-striping on cars. It brought in a few bucks on the weekend.

In shop class, we made rings, brass knuckles, and Maltese crosses and sold them. It gave me some money to buy smokes and wine or vodka along with clothes. The summer before eighth grade, in 1962, I began working on cars. I had built models a lot and worked on bicycles before, but this was a new venture. Most of my friends were older, and we began to put motors and transmissions in. We built one after picking the body up from the junkyard. We would run in and get the parts off old cars and just put it on the bill till we were ready or had it ready to take into town. We then got it to town and would drop in the engine. I had been doing some of this, so I had requests to do some clutch work on people's cars.

I then was also doing bodywork. My first was a '55 Chevy. They always rusted out above the headlights, so I would fix them. I had my permit to drive at fifteen, bought a 1940 Chevy for $25, and sold that after a year.

When I was sixteen, I got my license and bought a '50 Ford two-door. Baby blue with baby moons. I was an Hermano at the time. We were called a gang but got together because of all the fights we would get into with other gangs or towns. We had six hundred members in the state. I was sixteen, had a car, no school, and was making money.

I was working for the cab company as well as pinstriping and drawing, and at night, I would work at Jenni-O Turkey washing tanks. I was making about $90 a week, which was good in those years. During my stint with the cab office, I would sometimes do some of the runs bootlegging. We lived in a dry county, so through the cab company, we would do the supplying to those in need. Mostly whiskey and vodka, sometimes a little beer. It's amazing who would order this stuff. The people I worked with were fun, and we all got along. I did the dispatching at night from 11:00 p.m. to 7:00 a.m. I would go there after my job as a pizza cook at Crescendo Pizza.

I was nearing seventeen at the time and had quit my other job, which I had at the pool hall, cleaning at night for two hours or so. I also would cloth tables and fix cues when needed. But there was one problem. I kept getting busted for drinking, fighting, and avoiding arrest. I was already on probation for I don't know how many times. Well, this time I was going to go to the reformatory in Red Wing or take an offer to go into the army. I chose the army. I was given a choice of MOS and took aircraft maintenance. I liked motors and thought it would be something for when I got out. I had a hearing, and they waived my court date till after I was enlisted.

Even though I had had a good example and base, there were still some issues with my behavior. Dad walked the walk but still had trouble with his temper when it came to discipline. One time, buying shoes, he was happy he could get them for me. Like I said earlier, when you are young, you have no understanding. He picked out what would wear best and last for a while. He asked, "What do you think about these?" I said I hated them and would take them to a grinder the first chance I had. He blew up. Well, he asked.

Anyway, I got home, and he pulled off his belt and beat me with it till I was bloody from my waist to my heels. My mom turned white and almost passed out. This was worse than any other time. He was in a rage. My brother Mike also got it the same when he messed up. It was a common thing. I am not saying he was a bad person, but it is hard to understand and love someone like that. Here is where his growing comes in.

Before he passed, he wished he would have never been that severe and changed over the years. I watched this. He is forgiven. I understand the hurt he must have felt when he was glad to provide for his family, and I rejected it. We were all growing up together. This drove a wedge between us for a long time. From the time that nun smacked me around to this stuff, I had the idea anyone in authority was out to hurt you. I could only relate to outlaws and people that were treated this way. You had to always protect yourself. It was all about respect. I finally got my orders and was off to the bus to get sworn into the army in January of 1967.

CHAPTER 2

YOU'RE IN THE ARMY NOW

Yes, I was on my way with Kenny Bryant, a friend of mine. He had also quit school and had been in some trouble, so we went in under the buddy plan. He was in motor pool or vehicle maintenance; I was in aviation. We got to Minneapolis late at night, and the next day we were sworn in. It was winter and pretty chilly, but we were on our way to Fort Lewis, Washington. We took the Great Northern and made a stop in Montana. Well, of course, we had someone go to the liquor store and pick up something for us to drink on the way. We partied as long as we could, and finally, we were there. We got our clothes and were assigned to a barracks. It was what basic usually is: drills, marching, shooting, and stuff like that. Upon completion, I was sent to Fort Rucker, Alabama, for aircraft training. Kenny went somewhere else for vehicles.

I was in Alabama for a while, and then the orders came to go to Fort Campbell, Kentucky. Here I was assigned to the Sixty-first Assault Helicopter Company. We stayed with them for a short period. I was with the Fifty-eighth Aviation Detachment and was sent out to the airstrip with my plane and the 101st Airborne Division. Here we worked on our planes, and I did a lot of flying every day. I flew as a copilot almost every day to Atlanta. I became very familiar with flying and the aircraft. I was doing well. Of course, we partied a lot, but it never interfered with me taking good care of the planes. I had an excellent rating and was put in for a promotion before I went to Vietnam.

Then the orders came to go to Vietnam. I don't know if I was nervous or not. I don't think I gave it a lot of thought. There are always questions; of course, it's new. I didn't really have a girlfriend anymore. Patty Jay from Des Moines sent me one letter or two. Linda and I were done after I was ready to beat up this guy she saw before I left. They got him out of there and took my tire iron away so I didn't get busted the night I was supposed to leave. I learned that night and got over it. There is no woman worth fighting over. If they want to be with you, they will; if not, they won't. I thought that was great to conquer. Some people get bent out of shape, hurt themselves, and ruin their own lives because of it. It doesn't make sense to me. Just move on. Patty and I never heard from each other again. Of course, I had to hitchhike down to Iowa every time to see her. Oh well.

Well, off to Vietnam. I still can remember the worry on my folks' faces when I boarded the train to leave. I think now how my mom may have felt as well as my dad. They had lost two boys at a young age, and now I was going to a combat zone in another country. Dad was solemn and encouraging. Mom was holding back tears as I left.

Trains are where I have had some weird experiences. We were on this train, myself and another soldier, when we stopped for something. Anyway, there was a sandwich station there, and he went for a sandwich. I didn't want one and was sitting there when some guy from the back of the car came up and demanded I sit with him. I walked him back to his seat, and when I returned to mine, a lady sat by me to keep this guy from coming back to my seat. She went back to hers, and the next thing I hear is a blood-curdling yell from him in the back: "You gotta die! You gotta die!" I couldn't believe it.

Everyone just sat there to see if he would kill me or something. I thought, *Oh man, I gotta kill this guy first*. He came out from his seat, and I got up and put my hands on each seat across from the other. I was nervous at this point dealing with this drunk. Well, I just gotta come up and kick him in the throat when he gets closer. Halfway down the aisle, the back door swung open, and two conductors or something came in, tackled the guy, and dragged him off. A minute later, my friend came back and was proud of his sandwich. I said, "Dude, you gotta hear what just happened," and I told him he missed a good show.

Finally made it back to Kentucky and the airstrip. We picked up our planes and were on our way to Little Rock first. We refueled and were off to El Paso before going to California. I was flying copilot with Lt. Blunt. We had a stay for one night in El Paso, so we might as well go over to Juarez, Mexico, and party while we are here. So we did. We drank tequila till six a.m. and had to be back to our planes for takeoff. We got back, but not till after almost getting into a fight with a dozen big Mexican bouncers and being thrown in jail. We made it back, though. I was there with Norm, another crew chief. Getting back, we still could function and had brought another bottle of tequila with us for the road. We left El Paso and headed out towards the mountains on our way to Oakland, California. I remember going over the mountains at several hundred feet above what the ceiling was for our planes. We crossed them about ten miles an hour, with the wings shaking like they were ready to fall off.

Our planes were single-engine rotary engine jobs built by De Havilland from Canada in 1955 and 1957. We made a stop in Blythe, California, and it was around 110 degrees. Well, that other bottle of tequila was gone when we landed. On the way, I would go into the back and mix it with orange juice so the pilot wouldn't know. Well, he found out when we landed. We were forced then to stay in Blythe till morning when I could fly again. We finally made it to California and then were off on a merchant marine aircraft carrier to Nam.

It was interesting. We stopped in Hawaii and then the Philippines to pick up some pineapple juice. Upon leaving with the juice, we hit a terrible storm that had sixty-foot waves and started to flip that juice around. We had to block it up, or it would have destroyed our planes.

Coming into the country now, we stayed offshore a ways till morning. We got off the ship and onto a Navy troop carrier-type craft and were hauled to shore. We entered Vung Tau, which was an in-country R&R center. Well, we didn't know where our unit should be or where to go. We were issued an M-16 but given no bullets. We found out that the Sixty-first we were to be attached to had all been wiped out, and they were not around. I was sent to the Fifty-fourth and 255th Otter Air Service Company, and Dick Rather, Larry Mossier, Lt. Blunt, and the other two members of our detachment were sent to other places. I was assigned to a unit that hauled blue boys, we called it. We went and picked up the dead soldiers, and they were put in blue bags. Terrible, smelly job. I was there for a short time, then transferred to Bear Cat or Long Than. This is where the Ninth Infantry Division was. I was sent back again to Vung Tau for a short period till being transferred again to Dong Tam in the Mekong Delta.

Prior to this, I was flying to another spot and was with some special forces group. The gunship in the rear was shot down, and they had to go back and get them. I still had no ammo. They had taken my M-16 and given me an M-14, which was heavy and rusted fast. Anyway, they dropped me at Anderson outpost, where there were only about ten guys, and we were all underground. Right in front of your face was jungle brush, a really scary place. They came back and got me and took me to an Australian post, and that is where I finally got some ammo. It was the same as what was used for the M-60 on the gunships. After drinking beer and staying with them for a while, I was sent down the road and finally ended up at Dong Tam, moving the Ninth Infantry Division and helping build their base camp. It was a hot zone we were in; we had taken in rockets and mortar fire every night. We lived in tents and ate C-rations till the barracks were built and they had a mess hall, which was half a mile away on post. We were on the perimeter. Dick was sent to Phu Loi, and Mossier was sent up north to Kon Tum and Phu Bai area.

While I was at Dong Tam, I was chosen to fly some rescue missions as a door gunner. We flew to areas of some I know and some I don't know. We worked with some Marine units up north and Army units around Cambodia and Laos. Some wore no rank or had any ID. It was on one of these missions I had picked up my AK-47, and you could get the ammo from the prisoners or the dead. It was not the best job, but you felt you were serving your country, and you had no choice if you were going to survive. After the flying stint, I returned to Dong Tam for a short period and was sent back to Vung Tau for my last week or two in the country. Vung Tau was rarely hit, but they came under attack with a little fire before I left. I had gotten in-country at the start of the third Tet offensive, and there was action all over, it seemed. Vung Tau was pretty laid back.

During my tour, I did have some good Vietnamese friends. They taught me proper Vietnamese, and I got to where I could speak it rather fluently. I learned two dialects and did some interpreting. It wasn't the Vietnamese mixed with French like some learned. In Vung Tau, prior to my return to the States, I had known a Chinese fella who did some workaround for us. He taught me some Chinese, which I never got fluent in but could speak some. He had a Honda scrambler that he let me use on occasion when he was working, so I drove that around so we could go into the village there.

It was a few days before I left. We came under red alert and began taking a few rounds from rockets and mortars, nothing too serious in comparison to where I had come from. The only thing is in Vung Tau, they wouldn't let you have your weapon with you. They must have figured it was safe. Well, I never turned in any of my weapons; I had a stash. The NCOIC and I never got along, and he wanted my AK-47. Well, I didn't give it to him. I hid it, and when we came under attack, I had no assigned place to go, so I went out to the main bunker on the road. Here I found several new guys who didn't know how to load the M-60 machine gun or make a commo check. The sergeants in charge were sitting on a pile of boards telling jokes. This did not sit well with me.

Where I had come from, the VC would have come through and wiped them all out. I helped the guys make the comm check, showed them how to load and use the 60, then went down and locked and loaded on the sergeants in charge. I told them to do their job, or I'd take them out myself. They moved. I then went out to the airstrip to a small bunker by the revetments close to the choppers and planes. I was sitting there with two new guys, first-week in-country.

I had several rifles, my AK, a few grenades, a bag of weed, and about ten beers in my waterproof bag. The fireworks went on for a couple of hours, but nothing serious. The next day, I was called into the orderly room, and they gave me Article 15. This is something like a misdemeanor in court. The sergeant still demanded my AK, but I sold it to the sergeant in charge of the arms room. He was an E-7, and the one who wanted it was an E-6. I felt good about that; he didn't, though.

It was time to leave. I was to catch a flight to Cam Ranh Bay for the plane back. This was emotional. One of the guys there had ended up in the hospital for malaria. I didn't know him well but had seen him around, and it seemed he was teased quite a bit for some reason. He was a very quiet guy. I stopped and visited him before leaving and said goodbye to some of the others. It's like leaving your family. You get to know these people, similar to when you talk with one or have a friend, and the next thing you know, you are putting him in a bag because he has been shot or blown up. You just can't explain this stuff. It is a crying moment and at the same time happy when you leave.

We, of course, made it to Cam Ranh and caught the plane; we were on our way home. This is weird in a way; you expect things to be the same, but you just don't know what to think at the same time. But you are leaving. We flew for some time and landed for a short time in Tokyo, Japan, and then took off again. We landed in Oakland and got off the plane. What a relief. No firefights, red alerts, or rescue missions. Wow.

"Wow" was correct. After leaving and getting into the public, it was war again. Yes, with the people who were yelling for peace. You became ashamed of where you had been. They spit on you, called you baby burner, and would attack you. These were the love and peace people. You had to have civilian clothes, or they hounded you, short-changed you, spit in your food, threw perfume on you because you stunk, and called you a mother killer. It was much different than today. I was kicked off a bus because the love and peace people wanted to kill me, so the driver wouldn't let me on. I had to take a train to Stockton to visit a friend there instead. The cab driver charged me double. It wasn't a good time getting supposedly back home. Just ignorant people doing stupid things. Not the welcome you may think. I never expected anyone there just to go home.

Well, I was back, but it sure didn't seem like home. I wanted to go back to Vietnam. It was more peaceful. You at least had an idea who your enemy was. I finally got it set up and took a military flight to Andrews Air Force Base, then from there to Minneapolis by another Air Force flight. The cab ride to the bus station was interesting; he only stuck me double for the trip instead of triple like some would. I had my leave now and was glad to get back and see my brothers and sisters, mom and dad. They were grateful I made it back.

My dad took me down to the VFW for a beer. He thought I was just going to have a beer; well, I had the beer as a chaser for double shots of Jack Daniels whiskey. His eyes got big, and he said, "Well, we should get going." He saw what had happened and where I was going. Adjusting became very difficult. You just didn't fit in.

I was nineteen, and the people my age were just finishing high school, and I had already been to several other countries, seen war, and been degraded for it. Who can you relate to? I wanted to go back; I didn't care any longer. What purpose do I have? You couldn't even get a job at some places if you were a vet. They didn't want baby killers in their establishments. The only thing to resort to at the time was more drugs and drinking.

It seems you come to hate society as a whole. Do what you can to feel good was the game and rebel. I got worse and worse as time went on, from acid to shooting any type of dope you could get. There were dreams and memories constantly if you didn't stay stoned or tuned, as we called it. I hitchhiked around the country for a while selling pictures on the street. I traveled with Doug and Pat, a couple of friends, Tim, and my brother Mike for a while. We stayed under bridges, in alleys, wherever we could.

Prior to the traveling, I had lived in a commune in New Mexico with my girlfriend Suzie C. She was from England. When the heat was on and the police wanted to bust us, we all moved to Los Angeles. Sue and I stayed with some writers and still photographers in the moving picture group. They filmed *Wild Angels*, *Vampire Devil Bikers from Hell*, and those types of movies. I did get a job at Jerry's 66 gas station in Santa Monica. We were living in North Hollywood on Stanley Street, which was a long way. I had already lived on the strip across from Gazzarri's and didn't like it there. It was also too expensive. So we moved to Santa Monica to a little place. I had picked up a '58 Pontiac two-door hardtop then, so we had a car till it got towed. I had had a '55 Olds convertible prior to this, but it got vandalized, so I just sold it. Hitching was easier and cheaper.

Through the station where I worked, I met Goldie Hawn and Arte Johnson. They were working down the street on *Laugh-In*. They were fun, although I'm not impressed by what you do. I'm concerned about who you are. They were cool. My other roommate was the drummer for a band named Buffalo Springfield. He was okay. Anyway, we couldn't keep the place in Santa Monica, so we moved back to Bret and Carol's in Hollywood.

One day, Jerry, our neighbor, and my girlfriend went down to Malibu Beach to just smoke a joint, have one beer, and watch the ocean. Well, we had a little fire, and it was illegal to do that along with the drinking. In no time, we were surrounded by police, about eight or ten with billy clubs. They threw my girlfriend up against the car, and of course, we let them know how we felt about that. They didn't like our response, so they took Sue and sent her to Berkeley to her mom's because of her age and drinking. They left Jerry and me after Jerry calmed them down and talked them into not beating me to death. I then moved up to Berkeley and spent some time in the Bay Area. We went to Oakland for a bit and had a place next to a Black Panther meeting place. It was nice; you weren't bothered at all. We then decided to move back into the garage we had in Berkeley. It was cool; we had all the tapestries and incense burning all the time, you know, hippie days.

For some unknown reason, we moved back to Los Angeles, and Sue and I got into a big fight. Maybe I should say she did. She had a temper that I had never seen before. Throwing pans and knives at you? Well, not for me! I left, and she went back to Berkeley. I was on my way to Chicago. After being there a while, I went to Denver, which I kind of liked, especially Boulder. We hung out at the park and just stayed stoned and sold pictures. I then went back to Berkeley, and Sue had started going with some Pete guy, so I went down to Garden Grove, a few blocks from Disneyland. Here I met Lynette, but we all called her Sam. She was cute but dangerous. I mean trouble. Well, trouble could have been my middle name, I guess.

Sue wanted to get back with me, so she came to Garden Grove, and World War III broke out. She saw me with Sam, and it was on. I got up and left. Tim was with me, and we hitchhiked back to Minnesota with Sam. We returned to Willmar for a short time. I left Sam after a few weeks; she took off with a bike club. I knew I was done with her—too much trouble and a liar. She eventually got arrested and sent to prison, where she later died. To avoid getting too lengthy, I had taken some other trips to Indiana with Doug, and my last was to Spokane, Washington, where I finally got arrested, extradited, and sent to prison for accessory to a crime in Minnesota.

Here is where this gets interesting. Prior to this, I had been in Minneapolis. It was on a Wednesday. I was staying at this house with some people and had my own room. I went in there about two in the afternoon, and all of a sudden, I looked at my life and the person I had become. My parents had given me a cross, and I took this little thing with me wherever I went. But this day, I looked at it, and for the first time in my life, I was sorry. I believed in Jesus and God; we had gone to a Catholic school. But now something was different. I was sorry and went directly to Christ. I told Him if it wasn't for someone like me, He wouldn't have had to go to the cross. I broke down. I understand that scripture now: "Godly sorrow worketh repentance." It causes you to change. The coming Sunday, I was baptized in the spirit and didn't know what had happened. The Lord, though, had spoken to me, saying everything would be alright. I heard it like an audible voice; I knew it. I began speaking in tongues and didn't have an idea what it was, but I wanted to find out.

A few weeks later, I was in Washington, stoned and strung out on beer and downers with my girlfriend Lynette when I got busted because of the warrant for my arrest. We had not been living well, though, I must say. We were living in the woods off pine cone nuts, stolen produce, downers, and beer. She was standing there with my dog and my friend Gary Smith as they hauled me off. I was twenty-one, and she had just turned eighteen.

That was God's divine intervention. The beginning. I went from Washington back to Minnesota with two detectives and spent several months in solitary confinement. Here is where I went through the DTs and cold turkey off the drugs. That was quite the experience. I didn't know where I was, really. It got to a point where I couldn't recognize my mom. I was sentenced to five years. I only spent a few weeks at the St. Cloud reformatory before they transferred me to St. Peter Security Hospital for the criminally insane. I had become unpredictable and had hurt several inmates pretty badly. They sent me to the hole and transported me with two guards, chains, and a dog. The people I was in with at St. Peter had murdered several people and had no problem doing such things. I had no trouble with any, though. But I was so messed up mentally it was ridiculous. They took me in and gave me electroshock treatments five times to try to bring me back, and I must say it evidently worked. That was in 1972.

The whole point around this is that if you want to change your life, God is ready. Jesus Christ is not dead. The scripture says that "in no wise will He cast you out." I went to Him, but it took time and a willingness to change and learn about Him. I couldn't see this at the time. He has never left me, nor will he ever leave me. Every morning in basic training and throughout the day, we were constantly yelling, "Kill, kill, kill." We were programmed for this. It really doesn't make you a better person. But Christ does. Praise God. A lot of people were hurt and saddened by the person I used to be. Now that person is gone. That is freedom. The ability to have a choice.

There was a lady from Alamogordo, New Mexico, who took me to her house to meet her husband and family. They had a large ranch and horses, and it was right next to the mountains. My opinion at the time towards rich people was they were all greedy and loved their money. I was proven wrong by experience. They treated me with respect and as another human being. This began to whittle away my prejudices. Something I see now. Thank God. The things in the past I can't change, but I am forgiven. I got involved with God, and He got involved with me. Actually, I believe He has been there the whole time. With God, all things are possible.

My Catholic experience was not a good one. Not only were they strict, but they never told me God wanted my faith and respect. They wanted me to follow the sacraments, mass, stations of the cross, and catechism study. Never that I am saved by the blood of Jesus and that I can be led by His spirit. It was mass, confession, mass, confession, again and again, to be a good church member. The worst sin was against the church (their rules), not God. You were deemed a sinner till you died, then you might go to heaven after purgatory. No scriptural stuff at all. When Christ moved into me, I knew it. It was the best peace I have ever had. Better than any drug or drink. I now have an internal witness. I don't desire any drugs or drinking life at all. It is totally artificial to me. I can go anywhere if I choose to. I don't condemn anyone for what they do. Some I choose not to be around; they don't have what I'm looking for. Some are just too foolish.

What happened as I grew and finally got the victory over drinking, God put the right people in my path to teach and guide me on how to properly study the Bible. I found out it doesn't mean what you read. There is a picture behind the words. Words paint pictures, and a picture is worth a thousand words. My travels were moving about getting some experience, and a lot of it was unnecessary. I had created a lot of my own troubles through rebellion and being ignorant. Not stupid. Not having an understanding. Now I walk by faith, not by sight.

> That at that time you were without Christ,
> being aliens from the commonwealth of Israel,
> and strangers from the covenants of promise,
> having no hope in the world: But now in Christ
> Jesus you who sometimes were far off are made
> nigh by the blood of Christ. (Ephesians 2:12–13)

Reflections on Chapter 2

I had come out of the military, where I discovered war is real and saw the casualties that come along with it. People with their legs blown off, constant threats of attack, and how it becomes normal after a while. People in that country never get to go home because the battles are in their backyard. One day there is a building, the next, a large hole in the ground still smoldering. There is a certain smell to all this, and it is gross. Degraded and harassed when you return, there are memories that never fade. What is the purpose of all this?

Then a life that consists of wandering. What is the purpose of this? You may pray, but what are you praying for? Then off to prison. What for, what's the purpose? Correction or punishment?

After I had been sent to St. Peter from prison, I worked my way up to become part of the RAP program (resident assistance). There was a fellow named Bruce Peterson. He was thirty-seven in 1972 and had been there since he was eleven. Bruce couldn't read or write and was stuck there because of his rebellion. Bruce was cut up from knife fights and had been shot several times. They said he was trying to escape and running. I don't know how you get shot in the chest when running away, but that was their story.

Anyway, Norm Holby and I began to work with Bruce. He was beginning to read the Spot and Puff books. He began to spell his name, written like a child would write, of course. This opened a whole new world for Bruce. Prior to this, no one could control him. If you said you would meet him at a particular time and were late, he would stab you. Well, we explained things to him in a nice way, and he became more social.

One time, we asked to take him to this pond outside the gate to go fishing on a pass. They said, "Bruce! He's a runner." We got them to take a chance. Bruce went fishing with us, just a short walk to the little lake. Norm and I were sitting there, and we looked up, and Bruce was not to be seen. The next thing we heard was a scream coming from around the corner of the lake by the trees. It was Bruce. He came running around through the trees with a sunfish about a pound in weight. Bruce's first fish ever in his life. This was great. It makes me think Bruce, being hard to control, never got a lobotomy. This is something they did back in those days to some of the residents. You know what they used to say, "I'd rather have a bottle in front of me than a frontal lobotomy." Well, don't know where that came from, but on with the story.

It takes you back to when your dad took you fishing when you were young. This guy never had that. We began to see gratitude. This fellow had been locked up for twenty-six years, and he caught his first fish at thirty-seven in an institution. He was so excited he didn't know how to handle it. He didn't take the fish off; it was just hanging there on a hook. We showed him how, and we put it on a stringer. Time to get back now. When we arrived back, he was allowed to take it through the facility and show everyone his fish.

While Bruce was showing off his catch to the other inmates, we were working on the guards to let him clean it. You know, you catch it, you clean it. They said, "What? Bruce with a knife?" Well, they allowed it, and he cleaned his fish. We then pushed for more. Bruce caught it; well, let him eat it. Bruce wanted to give it to us in gratitude for taking him fishing. We had our own area upstairs with a little kitchen. They let us take Bruce up there and cook and eat it. After this, Bruce could be trusted. He went around and asked when your birthday was, and when it came, he would buy you a card and write "Happy B-day from Bruce" like a little kid. It was great. Better a card than getting stabbed.

What is the purpose of this? Well, I believe God had Bruce there for me to see a miracle take place in his life—a change. It helps me to understand gratitude in some things we take for granted. Like my folks said, "Get out of yourself and do something for someone else." In an institution? Yes, wherever you are. It helps with self-centeredness. I was released shortly after and sent to another facility for a few months and then released on the streets again. I have never forgotten the joy on Bruce's face after catching that fish. Norm had a heart attack, and Bruce was in there every day making sure he was all right. He had developed a concern for others. Isn't that great? Wow.

I was released shortly after Thanksgiving of 1972 and have never used drugs again since then. I did some drinking and quit in the fall of 1973, entered a professional chef training program, and went back for a while, partying and fishing. Prior to this, I went on the road in a duo playing music with a friend, Steve, who also played with me in the same band. We went on the road just before a Battle of the Bands concert, and the rest of the guys did take second place, which was good. We played from Iowa out to Utah, Green River being our last stop because the car broke down. I wired back for cash to get home because of the motel bill and no gas. Steve still plays and is accomplished in music. I dabble some but not regularly like in previous years.

During our stint in Green River, we met a fellow who had played with the Grand Ole Opry. This guy was good till he started drinking. That is why he was kicked out. How he ended up in Utah, I don't know. I was seeing the outcome of not controlling your life and habits. My dad once said, "If anything begins to control me, I get it out of my life." Good advice when you can hear it or take time to listen.

The purpose of things I have seen is so I could go back and find the good in them and discover God in the picture.

> All things work together for good to them
> that love God, to them who are the called accord-
> ing to His purpose. (Romans 8:28)

The purpose then, in reflection, is to get the message out concerning the love of God being there even when you don't think so. I had to reflect and discover God's purpose instead of always thinking I had been treated unfairly. Self-pity. Getting out of self and into God's plan for my life.

I like to define words; it helps me to understand. The definition of purpose is this: something set up as an end to be attained; intention. When going through certain things, you may think God is trying to kill you. Well, in a way. He wants the old you to pass away and come into a new and honest life. He mostly wants us to recognize Him as the one who has brought us through and into victory.

So then, what is my purpose? Well, to let people know God can and will bring you through. It is interesting how we choose certain people and lifestyles that have terrible consequences. It is breaking the patterns that revolve around what always seems right to us as individuals. We choose companions and things that cause us trouble and keep us in the same types of situations. I had to look at this stuff and seek after what I wanted in my life.

When I got busted, it was for a crime committed with another stoner. There were guns involved, and it was where a guy and his girlfriend almost got shot by us. Well, that was a consequence. Not planned; they never are—they just happen in that world. I looked back at some of the peace activists who wanted to kill me on that bus when I got back from Nam. They may have had time to think about how they treated people while demanding peace and love. They are the idiots. I am healed through forgiveness. Why do I need to feel pain in the emotions because I am rejected for something I have no control over? Same as today with some of these protests. They burn down another man's store because they want something. Peace and respect.

> Surely mercy and goodness shall follow me
> all the days of my life. (Psalm 23:6)

If we sow good, we get good, but at the same time, we get opposition. Look at Jesus. His came from religious people who were judgmental and critical. That is a system. You know, "I'm not that bad. They are worse than me." Self-righteous. They are in a sad place and fearful.

It has been many years now, but when I got out of prison, jails, and institutions, God still accepted me. The only thing with people is they have to see consistency. My parents had three of us in prison at one time. We were each in different ones. They were hurt not based on how we made them look but on what they knew we were doing to ourselves. They would even tell you that. They said, "It is not how we look but how you look." Why could they say that? Well, I examined this. Because as I mentioned in an earlier section, they knew they set an example. It was in them.

How could David say, "Goodness and mercy shall follow me"? He showed respect for God's people and stuck with it. Even though you didn't want David looking for you, he never built the temple. The wise man did. Solomon. I had to become a wise man. In the past, I called Pat BC. If you gave me too much change at the register, I would keep it." Now I give it back. Why? The short in the till could cost the person working there part of their check to make it up. God has changed my nature and desire. It is an internal witness. The only way to peace.

CHAPTER 3

IS THERE LIFE AFTER DEATH

I WILL BEGIN WITH LIFE. LIFE is "the sequence of physical and mental experiences that make up the existence of an individual." So I had to look at life. What would it be like not to be angry, vengeful, and always assuming something? I had never lived a life like that because it was never an experience. I had been in trouble from an early age—war, firefights, and back before my classmates had finished school. I was in fights and battles with other gangs. Life was survival, not living. Need a car? Steal one.

I recall one time when I wanted to move back to Los Angeles because I couldn't find a good party. I stole a fire truck. I didn't know it at the time until we were stopped in Missouri. It was in 1970, and they didn't have the communications of today, and I talked my way out of it. I told the police we were on a test drive and had to get it back.

When I was in seventh grade, we used to sell candy, gum, and rubbers to the kids. Of course, we stole it all from a candy company. We sold protection for lunch money—from us, of course, or we would beat them up and wreck their bike. Trouble, trouble. If someone looks at you wrong, just punch them in the face. Couldn't take criticism. This was one area where people responded mostly because they didn't know who they were. What kind of approval was I looking for? Can we see ourselves as our friends see us and believe it? These are all weird questions, I guess.

So where does death come in, in relation to life? Death is the loss of life. My old life was based on how I saw things, based on my emotions toward my experiences. From the time that nun beat my hands with that pointer rod, I knew everyone in authority was out to get me. Well, get them first. Many of the other situations that happened I had created myself because of what had been done to me and how I was treated, especially in the Catholic school. Even with the religion they taught, it was all made up and interpreted. I never knew the love of God. It was rules, law, and purgatory. I had to overcome religious ideas, judgments, and criticism from people who didn't know even what they were doing. Even after my time in the service, I didn't start the war. I wasn't responsible. You know there is an old song that says, "Let there be peace on earth, and let it begin with me." I had to get this peace inside me first. When I received the spirit, a change took place that was an ongoing process. The change didn't happen overnight. If it did, it was the longest night I ever had. This is why I have gone back and reviewed my life and events to look for an understanding concerning not my behavior but what I must do about it.

In some cases, I never had feelings of guilt. I was guilty. First, I had to quit living in the emotional realm of feelings. This doesn't mean I don't have them; I am not governed by them, especially when I got the feeling I was responsible for starting the war. Maybe also in relation to how many people we put into bags that were shot or blown up. Yes, I don't like to see this. It takes letting go and finding my purpose. I must first discover the solution to the problem. I had to let go and let God. Carrying pain in a way also can fall into a category of pride. It is also a way of getting attention. I noticed that we become a product of what we feed and think about. Some stuff is very difficult. It is like visiting a monument over and over to feel the pain. It is letting go. Even some things we have done to others—and I have done some terrible things, and they were on purpose. Do I need to carry that around forever? I don't think so. The Bible states that God does not remember them. He says, "Your sins and iniquities I will remember no more." Religion is always bringing up how we always fail. How can I succeed if I'm focusing on failure? Doesn't make any sense. I am forgiven, and God isn't thinking about that.

YE OLDE MILL INN

Going back to when I finally went to Christ, a voice came and said it would be alright. Then I got busted. Divine intervention. He saved my life—or should I say, He gave me one. Yes, and now I have more of a purpose than I did before. All I did was shoot dope, drink, and smoke weed. It just seemed like the thing to do, but God was working under it all to deliver me and give me some peace. I now have life.

My experiences now, with spiritual help and power, are the ability to go in hope and expectation. I never even got this in the Catholic Church. Here is where I see my dad's example and sticking to what he did. Practiced what he preached, as they say. Over the years, he changed and brought himself under control. He avoided situations that would deter him from his course and priorities. This was something to begin to get me to practice a new way of life. I am careful of the people I want to get involved with. I don't dislike people, but why try to have a life with someone who doesn't want it? Some have no desire to change. They create turmoil and trouble for me to deal with that I don't have to. I now have boundaries. It is learning from the past and then learning to hear God's voice. Sometimes it is a gut feeling. I am not obligated to fail.

Yes, there is life after death. It comes when you give up the old life and ways. It took a willingness to seek and check things out and finally find peace. There are still everyday situations, but now I have more knowledge of God, His word, and some experience where He will not fail me.

If He did this for me, He will do it for you. Thank You, Jesus.

CHAPTER 4

THE CRUX OF IT ALL

WHEN PUTTING THIS WRIT TOGETHER concerning my life and experiences, there had to be a purpose and a goal. A large portion of the previous chapters were written years ago. But what about the present and the later years? Throughout the past, I have had girlfriends pass away; one hung herself, and I lost another with her brothers in a car rollover. I had shock treatments five times in the early '70s. Many friends overdosed and died from drinking-related problems.

In the '80s, we lost everything and were shunned by our church friends. This was after becoming a Christian and working in the ministry with Bible studies. I have had radio broadcasts that I have been kicked off of because they weren't theologically sound for some of the denominations. My daughter was diagnosed with an incurable health issue (she is in her forties and doing well). I lost our house, and all savings, and we were living out of our car. I kept faith in God and believed Jesus Christ was true, the Word was true, and God would restore all things.

I have been divorced. I started a sign company when I was nearly homeless. I lived in a sixty-dollar-a-month room where people were getting stabbed and drunk all the time. I moved up to a three-hundred-dollar-a-month efficiency and kept plucking away. God opened doors and gave me ideas and opportunities. I have had several body shops and bike shops working on Harleys and English bikes. I kept studying, always learning, and working. For a while, I was a barber at home. (God put a barber in my path to teach me, and I took it, so I also cut hair for a while.) I ended up welding LP tanks and painting them till the company closed.

MEDIA PRESS
PASS
Authorized Media Personnel
NAME: PAT KINNET
SIGNATURE
EXP: 01-2005
№ 1PK04
This press pass is valid for media events
BIKES
n' dolls
For those who Live to Ride... The Complete Cycle Magazine
21441 N. 3rd Ave
Phoenix, AZ 85027
TEL: (623) 879-6684
FAX: (623) 879-6683

I got involved with carpet and ceramic tile construction, doing roofs, and building churches. I opened my first tattoo shop in 1993 and sold out in 2007. During this time, I was still doing teaching tapes on Scripture for truckers and doing conferences. For a while, I was repairing antique clocks and doing veneering and furniture in another garage shop I had. I airbrushed T-shirts and designed banners for bands, along with posters and album covers. What I did was practice things that would further me. I learned plumbing and wiring and drilled water wells for a bit. Life is about learning and application. I spent time trying to always carry my own weight. I couldn't tell you what was on TV for over fifteen years. I was too busy.

I will be reaching a point; this is not to brag or belittle anyone; there is a purpose for this. I also studied medicine for around nine years and was into massage and homeopathy, along with electrotherapy and acupuncture with basic chiropractic moves and adjustments. (I did this for free at the tattoo shop. I felt I had hurt enough people and wanted to do something good for them.)

I also finished with honors from a course in customizing out of Newport Beach, California, and took a small engine course for something to do. I attended the St. Cloud Business College for bookkeeping and accounting but never took the test to become a CPA. This helped me with keeping order in my businesses, and my dad also helped me learn this. He taught me to write letters when I was writing to magazines and record companies in relation to promoting my artwork. I kept up with the learning. That is enough at this point.

I have actually a ninth-grade education. I flunked everything in school, not because I was stupid but because I didn't care. Today I am seventy-five years of age. I began these ventures when I was twenty-three. One of my first trainings was auto reconditioning. I had had airplane mechanics through the service, but now I had to start doing something. I took the GED twice. I flunked the first time because I was bored and it was too hot.

My dad used to always say you need drive and consistency. I am 100 percent convinced that God can and will open doors and a way for us to succeed if we allow Him. This doesn't mean we will be the best in the world, but it is learning that we can accomplish something. I found by reading, opening the ears, and listening, we can go a long way. I do not have the personality to just do nothing and sit around. There is something here worth noting. As you progress, certain people will fall by the wayside—that's life.

When we serve God, we give Him what He wants: respect and thanksgiving. My folks would not allow us to say "I can't." That's a great thing to understand now, for I can do all things through Christ who strengthens me. In the process of growth, I discovered if we don't forget about others, we can keep peace and a purpose. My purpose is not just to make a good living or think I have learned so much and done so much that now I am a know-it-all. It is to enjoy life and be an asset in the life of another. It is about being the same with or without. This is contentment. A person's value is not based upon what material things they have or their position in society. It is based upon God and our relationship with Christ. He wants us to succeed so we can be an asset to His kingdom. Having finances to be a blessing.

How then do I write books? Well, first, I read. Second, I still remember basic English principles and how things are written. Then do it till you get it. Do I have it? I don't know. I just do it. As the scripture says, "As for me and my house, we will serve the Lord."

I hope you have discovered some good principles through this writing. Move forward and have a prosperous, satisfied life. With Jesus Christ, you only have a future.